WAILING WALL

WAILING WALL

A MOTHER'S MEMOIR

deedra climer

INKSHARES

For *JACK*, the reason for all my stories
and
for Fanoona, who is enough all by herself

Published by Inkshares Inc., San Francisco, California
www.inkshares.com

Edited and designed by Girl Friday Productions
www.girlfridayproductions.com
Cover design by Mumtaz Mustafa

ISBN: 9781941758113
Library of Congress Control Number: 2015938846

First edition

Printed in the United States of America

Prologue

A stone wall, more than two millennia old, stands in Jerusalem, all that is left of what was once a great temple. In the Muslim tradition, Temple Mount is considered the destination of Muhammad's Night Journey and the place where he ascended into heaven. For Christians, the plaza of the temple is where Jesus prayed and chased away the merchants for desecrating a holy place.

Temple Mount is the holiest ground in Judaism, a place of pilgrimage and prayer. Jews come to this wall to publicly mourn its destruction by the Romans. Today, people from many faith traditions all around the world come to the Wailing Wall to pray. Some write their prayers on slips of paper and tuck them in the cracks in the ancient stone and mortar.

I started writing this story on the back of an envelope the day my son died. I shared pieces of my story on social media—and later in public readings—looking for a place my sorrow fit among the other stiff and yellowed pieces of paper in the Wailing Wall.

Public mourning saved my life.

This is my lamentation.

1

It's near midnight and I'm kneeling on filthy white tile with my face inside a toilet bowl. The bleak fluorescent light shows smears and stains I would rather not see. My body lurches, then rids itself of the ginger ale I forced down an hour ago. I sit back on my heels, try to breathe through the next heave. But my spit is thick, and the air is sour. I heave again.

Grimy metal walls with peeling red paint separate me from the other women in this rest area bathroom. From the next stall someone says, "Too much to drink, hon?"

Her voice is sweet in the way only a Southern woman's can be. Blessing your heart and cutting your throat at the same time. I can see pink rhinestoned sandals and a fresh pedicure under the wall.

"Fuck off," I say, but my words are indecipherable through the sounds coming from my body. I wipe my face on the sleeve of my shirt and lean against the wall. Through a crack, I see her apply lipstick, blot it, and leave without washing her hands.

The rest area is just outside of Nashville, and, unlike my home in southern Michigan, the air feels like a wet blanket even though it's the first day of May. Most of the travelers who have stopped are walking their dogs or taking a smoke break. I imagine they are on their way to someplace pleasant—a reunion or maybe a rock concert. But not me. I am traveling to bury my only son.

Back in the car, my husband, Bill, checks the weather and returns texts that came while he was driving. He's driven most of the trip without talking as is his way. He's my rock. He knows me and all the dirty details that come with me. He never blinks when I visit Memphis where I sleep in my ex-husband's garage apartment. He doesn't growl when I ask how much money we have in savings because one of my children needs help to get out of the crisis du jour. He is my safe place.

"Who texted?" I ask as Bill scrolls through the messages.

"Everyone," he says, looking at his phone and running his fingers over his long bushy beard. "They just want to know how you are."

"Well," I ask him, "how am I?" Is it pity I see in his eyes as he stares at me? "Do I seem normal?"

I have no idea how I'm doing. Since we left the farm in Michigan, I've spent the ride floating in the darkness of my own mind. I feel nothing. Not even numbness. I wonder if I still exist at all.

"You are doing fine," he tells me. "As well as anyone would expect."

I raise the lever to recline my seat and stare at my sixteen-year-old daughter, Claudia, in the backseat. She's wedged between luggage with her earbuds in and her eyes closed. Her breathing is rhythmic except for a whimper. Is she sleeping? I should talk to her. Soothe her. But the last time we spoke was last night, just minutes after I had gotten the call. I met her in the lobby coming out of a movie and told her that her brother was dead. What can I say to her now that would be of any consequence?

· · ·

It's after two a.m. when we pull into the long driveway of Noè's house. A fire is burning in the pit, and people are standing in the flickering shadows. Standing. Waiting for me—the mother of the deceased. I know they are here in support, but I feel like a freak show. *I won't break down,* I think. *As long as I don't have to look at them.*

Claudia opens her car door, and the interior light thrusts me into view. I can't hide any longer. I make my way through the line of hugs and tears and hold back the dark and violent thing curdling in my belly. As I get closer to the house, it crawls through my chest and escapes, animalistic and raw, into the night.

Bill whisks me inside and gives me a glass of water. Tables are piled with a blend of Mexican and Southern grieving food. *Pan dulce.* Pozole. Macaroni and cheese and more fried chicken than I've ever seen in one place. In the corner of the kitchen, a folding table holds fresh flowers and a lit prayer candle with the Virgin de Guadalupe. In the middle, a framed picture of Joshua lounging on top of his Dyna Super Glide Harley-Davidson. His arms are crossed, and there's a satisfied smile on his face.

Others have brought pictures from their personal albums, and there are some I've never seen. Josh boxing with his best friend, Miguel, at four years old. The grimace on his face looks like that of a serious boxer, but his dad's boxing gloves cover his arms up to the elbows. A few years later in an orange Boy Scouts T-shirt and cap, beaming at his new baby sister, Kelsi, as she lies on a blanket and pumps her fists into the air. At the Tennessee State soccer tournament and, later, at the sports banquet receiving an award for most valuable player. In his high school cap and gown with his hair in cornrows.

Noè shuffles out of his bedroom in his slippers and pajama pants and stands beside me in front of the memorial. He puts his arm around my shoulder, and we stand silently side by side.

The smell of food is overwhelming—I am woozy and I hope he doesn't speak.

Yesterday, when the police officers came to his door with the saddlebag from Joshua's motorcycle, he collapsed to his knees. Soon after, he identified our son's body. That image sours my stomach, and I pinch my eyes shut to drive it away. My heart breaks for Noè, and, at the same time, I'm glad it was him instead of me.

"He's beautiful, ain't he?" Noè finally says.

I nod. He is the most beautiful thing I've ever done.

2

In 1949, the Russians started building nuclear weapons and my
mama was born. Any connection between the two has yet to be
proven. After Mama, two more children were born, and, when
the youngest was seven and my mama seventeen, I came along.
My sister, Jessica, followed four years later. Through most of my
childhood the lot of us lived in a house with white asbestos sid-
ing, two small bedrooms, and one bathroom.

Memphis was a different city back then. We lived in the
working-class part of town where children played outside until
the streetlights came on, and most every house had two parents.
It was light-years away from the places we lived later on as Mama
tried to disengage from her parents and drug us, as my mamaw
would say, from pillar to post.

When I was a year old, my mother went on a joyride with
folks who'd had too much to drink. The ride ended with her body
thrown from the car and James Road coated with her blood. My
grandfather went to the hospital every day after work for months
to be with his daughter, who was lying comatose with broken
bones and a traumatic brain injury. I stayed at home with my
mamaw and sat in her scrap box while she sewed choir robes

for the church. By the time Mama came home from the hospital, she was addicted to painkillers on top of the devastating effects of the brain injury she had sustained. I've often wondered how I responded when she walked in the door. I hadn't seen her at all for months. Then, to see her with a shaved head and stitches that went from her left ear around to her right temple? I must have been scared. Perhaps my terror—along with the distance that came from being separated from her for so long—was the beginning of our painful relationship. Perhaps, if the car wreck had never happened, she would not have turned to drugs at all.

When I was old enough to ask about him, Mama told me about the day she met my father. It was just after the Fourth of July, 1966. My grandmother had started to have dark days and stood at the porcelain sink washing the same brown melamine bowl long past what it needed and staring out the window. Mama painted black eyeliner in thick strokes around her eyes, slicked her dark hair into a Cleopatra, and pulled on tight pedal pushers. Her mother didn't notice when Mama slipped out, careful not to let the screen door slam behind her.

Memphis in 1966 had cotton trains rolling down the tracks above Riverside Drive leaving a trail like snow behind them. Cotton fibers floating through the air and sticking to the sweaty skin of ladies shopping downtown, and paddleboats nodding along the choppy Mississippi River. Mama said teenagers with nothing better to do gathered at the boat docks. Mama sat on a brick wall with bare feet dangling, swigging warm beer from a bottle in a brown paper bag.

Standing next to her was a redheaded boy, a few years older than she was, wearing a tight white T-shirt with the sleeves rolled up. A handmade tattoo on his left forearm read "Lucky."

"Want a hit?" She extended the bottle in his direction. In those days, Mama introduced herself as Dago, a nickname an aunt had given her because of her dark hair and olive complexion. Mama embraced the name—thought it sounded tougher than Vicky. Only the boy wasn't impressed. He took the bottle and poured the last of the beer on the ground. Told her she was too young to be drinking.

Lucky was half of a set of identical twins known in the neighborhood for fighting dirty and drinking too much. They had enlisted in the Marines together, just like they did most things, and boarded a plane for Da Nang two weeks after they turned seventeen. Home was a clapboard shack behind Rex's Pharmacy just off the highway.

Mama said Lucky's mother spent her days in a straight-back chair on the front porch staring out at what might have been a yard but was instead gravel and broken bottles. Tucked inside the pocket of her housedress was a pint of vodka and her teeth in case company should come by. She kept these things in her dress for her own easy access and so no one else could find them: Not her boys, who stole nips of vodka before they even had their school teeth. Not the Department of Children's Services that came in the middle of the night and took her daughter. And not her caseworker, who visited without warning and caught her without her teeth more than once.

Not one to be thwarted, Mama asked, "How'd you get that name anyway? Are you lucky?"

"I don't know. Am I?" He took a last, long drag off his Marlboro, then thumped the butt toward the water, where it landed in good company.

Lucky had been to Vietnam, which officially made him a badass in Mama's book.

Lord knows, Mama loves a badass.

.   .   .

Mama says we lived with my daddy until I was four and Jessica was newborn, but I don't remember it. When we weren't living with my grandparents, it was Mama, Jessica, and me with whatever boyfriend Mama was hooked up with at the moment. Growing up, I spent half my time wanting to be just like my mama. She was so worldly. I wanted to know the grown-up things she knew. I wanted to understand about sex and drugs like she did.

The other half of the time, if I looked at her too long, she would start to consume me. If I didn't catch myself in time—before my edges started to fade—I feared we would merge. That I would become just another part of her and none of myself at all.

The first time I knew about Mama and drugs, I was six years old. Now that I'm an adult, I understand it better than I did then. At that time, I was just a scared little kid with pee pants.

We lived in Northaven, a new subdivision where many of the lots were still just red dirt with white pipes sticking out of the ground. Mama and her latest boyfriend, Eddie, slept in the big bedroom. Jessica and I slept in the room across from Mama and Eddie. The third bedroom was just blankets on the floor so if any of their friends needed a place to sleep, they could sleep there. But they rarely bothered and just lay out in the living room, crossed over each other like cut logs.

Mama and her friends did grown-up things after we went to bed. Mama said that after we were asleep it was her time and she warned us not to get out of bed.

One night when I just couldn't hold it any longer, I got out of bed. Careful not to wake Jessica, who was still in diapers, I cracked the bedroom door open. Mama and her friends were in the kitchen. To make it to the bathroom, I would have to get past them. How badly did I have to pee? Was there anything in the room I could use instead of going all the way to the bathroom? I had already peed a little in my panties just to let the pressure off.

I *really* needed to go, I decided, and inched out of the bedroom hugging the wall to the bathroom.

If they saw me out of the bedroom, Mama would get mad. Eddie too. The adult-size T-shirt I was sleeping in reached almost to the floor, so I had to hike it up a little to walk. All the grown-ups were in plain view, but no one noticed the kid with long, stringy hair skulking in the hallway.

". . . into that car. So I know she had enough money to pay for it." Eddie was standing by the stove waving a spoon in the air while he talked.

"Is it ready yet?" Mama asked.

"No," Eddie answered quickly without looking at Mama.

"Anyway, when they came back to get the car, I asked him about it," Eddie kept talking. "Hey, where's that script?"

Mama passed him a little bottle that looked like the ones my cough syrup came in. While he finished his story, he bent the spoon into an *S* shape, then poured a drop from the bottle into the bowl. Then, he hung it over the side of the pot of boiling water.

Mama looked upset. She was sitting on the floor close to Eddie with her arms around her knees. She didn't take her eyes off him and the spoon.

"Is it ready?" Mama seemed mad it was taking so long. She stood up and dug into her back pocket and pulled out a needle. I had seen these before lying around the house, sometimes with a little bit of blood inside. Mama handed it to Eddie, then sat down at the table and tied a scrap of material around her left arm.

Eddie peeled the paper off of a cigarette butt and laid it in the spoon. Then, he put the needle down on the filter and pulled the liquid from the spoon up into the needle, held it up to the light, thumped it a few times, and then did it again.

Mama's long fingernails were tapping on the table, and she was making fists with her left hand. Eddie walked to the table and pulled over a chair with big orange-and-brown flowers.

He pressed the needle against Mama's arm. I could see the blunted end of the needle make a dimple in Mama's arm and bust through her skin with a pop. Mama's head dropped back against the chair, and she saw me frozen in the hallway.

Mama smiled a lazy smile, then closed her eyes as a drip of blood rolled down her arm, onto her pinkie, and landed in a red blossom on the dingy yellow linoleum.

3

I had my first child, Kimberly, when I was seventeen, though I didn't feel like a mother until much later. I got pregnant the same year my mother, my sister, and I moved out of my grandparents' house and into a two-bedroom town house in a section 8 complex fifteen or so miles away.

It was the farthest I had ever lived from my grandparents.

Though I didn't fully understand it, my pregnancy carried the shame of generations. My grandmother had conceived my mother out of wedlock, just as my mother had conceived me. There was an unspoken rule that I should not be seen by my grandparents while I was pregnant, and this carried a loud message of disappointment and rejection.

Since I was not yet of age to have my own case, the welfare department added me to my mother's case as a "pregnant dependent." Though I didn't have a steady boyfriend, the facts of my baby's paternity had never been discussed. So when the caseworker asked, I was taken aback. My baby was mine. What difference did it make who else participated in making it happen?

"I don't know who the father is," I said.

The caseworker laid down her pen and looked at me. "A father is obligated to provide financial support for his child. It is not the state of Tennessee's role to support children born out of wedlock."

A father is obligated, I thought. I hadn't had enough exposure to fathers to consider what they were obligated to do.

"Do you understand that if you lie about the identity of the father of your child, you could be subject to a fine, imprisonment, or both?"

"Um, yes," I replied, briefly considering whether I should make up a name or offer her a list of possible suspects. The caseworker showed me where to sign, and Mama and I were on our way.

Leaving the Department of Human Services, Mama lit a Marlboro 100, took a deep drag, and let it hang from her lips. "You ain't pregnant by a nigger, are ya?"

Mama's question made it clear the only acceptable answer was no, but I really *didn't* know who my baby's father was. As the child of an addict, I learned to substitute the love and acceptance I didn't get at home with sex. Sometimes my partners were white. Sometimes they were black. In later years, they would also be Latino, Asian, and African. There was always someone who wanted me, at least for a while.

After Kimberly was born, we lived with Mama for eight months before it became clear that my daughter's father was, indeed, black. My attempts to brush her hair into a ponytail resulted in tiny springs of curl popping out all over her head. Her eyes went from gray to a beautiful milk chocolate with flecks of gold. Even after it was obvious to everyone else, though, my family felt that never talking about the "situation" would just be easier on all accounts.

The next several years were complicated as I searched for the place where my family's worldview and mine could comfortably coexist. I drew boundaries for how I expected them to behave around my daughter. And, if I felt the conversation was disrespectful and damaging to my daughter's spirit, I would leave. Whether she was old enough to understand the words or not, I believed she would sense that something about her was unacceptable, even as they smiled and cooed at her. With time and a lot of tears, conversations and word choices improved, even if opinions did not.

Kimberly was diagnosed with a profound hearing impairment at eighteen months old, and the two of us lived off of her monthly Social Security Disability check in Midtown Memphis. Our apartment was in what was once preserved as a historic home but was now converted into four shabby apartments. Our hardwood floors showed layers of paint and were so warped a child not yet steady on her feet often stumbled. What was once a gallant fireplace was now bricked in. Since it was the eighties—I painted it seafoam green.

Many of the other homes in the area were torn down, and the neighborhood lost the value it once had. Rather than historic Southern homes with balconies and magnolia trees, the neighborhood was now filled with apartment buildings to house the lowest-income residents of the city—immigrants, the homeless, and, of course, single mothers. A block from where we lived was "the track," where sex, drugs, and money changed hands all day and night. The Memphis heat is oppressive, and we slept with our windows open, since we didn't have air-conditioning. Only wrought iron burglar bars protected us from the world outside.

That is where we lived when I met Noè.

.   .   .

Noè was nineteen and the most beautiful man I had ever seen. He was tall and slim, and his green eyes were striking against his caramel-colored skin. His angular features showed that his

Mexican indigenous heritage ran deep. My grandmother had bought a pocket-size Spanish-English dictionary at a yard sale when I was twelve, and she and I had spent years throwing out Spanish word challenges to each other. Naturally I felt prepared to strike up a conversation when I saw that handsome Spanish-speaking man at a bowling alley. His English and my Spanish were about on par, and, when he invited me back to his house for a drink, I assumed we were having beer. Instead, we had orange juice.

Less than a year before I met him, Noè swam the Rio Grande to come to the United States. He told the story of climbing a river rock and watching the body of another young man float by him: this left me even more in awe of him. In Chicago, his two older brothers had already settled and started families, and he had made his way there to work and send money to help support his parents, disabled brother, and two younger sisters back in central Mexico. Then, a job offer came, and he moved to Memphis to work fifteen-hour days in the kitchen of a Chinese restaurant for a hundred dollars a week, three meals a day, and a bedroom in a small duplex with the other kitchen help. The owners of the restaurant renamed him Tommy because his name was too hard to pronounce.

I wish I could say we married out of love but necessity is likely a better word. He needed a green card, and I needed someone to help me find my way. I admired him for his courage and for what he had done to help his family, and I thought he could make my life hurt less.

.   .   .

Joshua was born three years after we married. Having come three weeks early, he was a scrawny little thing with a cap of black hair and dark-blue eyes. Kimberly, now five, was quite a "little mama" to him and was always ready to fetch a diaper or let me know if Joshua seemed unhappy. She was so attached to her little brother, I had to convince her to leave him long enough to go to school.

There were so many things that kept me from feeling like an apt parent. Kimberly's hearing impairment brought communication challenges. There was also my age and the fact I lacked any knowledge of how to help my children feel loved and safe in the world. I wanted to be a good mother, but my only context for that was *not* doing what my mother had done. And that was not enough.

For the first several years, I approached parenting as a list of tasks to complete. Tasks I failed at more often than not. From Kimberly's perspective, I imagine she thought of her mother as the person who fed her, bathed her, walked her to school, and yelled at her when she misbehaved. Rare were times of cuddling or reading a book at bedtime.

Having a new baby in the house changed things for me. I was older and slightly more wise when Joshua was born. I had a husband and wasn't alone in managing the household. But he was a boy, and that forced me to examine the parenting stories that existed in my head. From my own childhood, I learned that girls were shameful, emotional, and smelly. Girls shouldn't make waves or speak out of turn. They should use their bodies and sexuality to get what they needed from others. And it was the mother's job to teach them these things. But what about boys?

Having no history of how mothers and sons interacted, I reimagined what I thought I knew about parenting. Maybe, with a boy, I didn't have to worry so much that he would cause a scene or get a bad reputation. Maybe it was okay for him to show emotion, be angry, and speak his mind. And if it was okay for Joshua, maybe it was okay for Kimberly as well. Maybe it was even okay for me.

This realization gave me a chance to relax. To let my children be human with the wide range of feelings and behaviors that go with that. With time, my anxiety lessened, and I had a few parenting wins. Even if I didn't quite know what to do with the information, I constructed a new definition for "mother."

By the time Josh turned two, our immaturity and the cultural differences became too much, and Noè and I separated. On my own again, I had no income other than Kimberly's disability check, an apartment I couldn't afford, and two children to support. I was overwhelmed and afraid, and, looking for relief, I sent my children away.

My mother admonished me with disgust in her voice. "No matter where I was or what I was doing, I always kept you with me." In her mind, that was a *good* thing. But I knew how much it hurt to have a mother so ill-equipped to parent. Not only was there the matter of being able to feed and clothe my children, anxiety fueled my fear that, like my mother, I would lose my mind and hurt them—or, at best—not be able to protect them. The only way I knew they were safe was if they were not with me.

I gave custody of Kimberly to her father. His family loved and accepted Kimberly the moment they found out about her. They took her on family vacations and bought her Easter dresses and did all the things I imagined normal families did. Compared to the mess I was making of my life, living with her father seemed like the obvious choice.

Joshua's godparents—Noè's oldest brother, Chava, and his wife, Gloria—cared for Joshua. After several months, when I had secured a place to live, found a job, and bought a car, I was ready to bring my children home. Chava and Gloria had seen their care of Joshua as a family supporting one another in times of need. Kimberly's father, however, petitioned to get custody of her through the juvenile court system, and she lived with him for seven years.

The pain of being apart was intense for us all. Joshua and Kimberly missed each other terribly, and they both sobbed when our weekend visitations ended. Every time I picked her up at her father's house in the suburbs, I felt more incompetent as a parent. Every time Kimberly asked why Josh lived with me and she didn't, I was destroyed.

Over twenty-five years later, I still wonder if I did the right thing. I regretted it immediately, for my own selfish reasons. Who was I, after all, without my children? Kimberly came back to live with me when she was fourteen, but it took years afterward and lots of blood, sweat, and tears for us to become friends. To her, what I had done felt like abandonment. Sometimes it felt the same way to me.

Kimberly stayed in Memphis when we moved to Michigan. But after her son, Michael, was born, her relationship with his father deteriorated, and she moved to Michigan to live with us while she sorted out what was next. On the night I got the call that Joshua had died, Bill and I had taken Michael, now five, to dinner while Kimberly sat for the Michigan State Board Examination for Cosmetology. After passing the test, she'd run herself a bubble bath and lit candles to celebrate when I arrived with the news.

Naked, she ran to her phone and texted her brother furiously, not believing he was dead and knowing it was true at the same time. She had texted with him earlier that day, joking about beating up a girl who broke his heart. After an hour or so without a reply, she packed her car with everything she owned. Losing Joshua broke her heart in all the places it was weakened by life. When we went to Memphis for the funeral, she went back to Memphis to stay.

4

Instead of being safely cocooned in my bed, I wake up on a couch in a living room with buttercup-colored walls and white lace curtains. A concrete fountain bubbles in the corner.

It is real. This is not a nightmare.

The chair where Bill slept is empty. Three of Joshua's five sisters—Claudia, Kelsi, and Bella—are on the front porch. I'm alone on Noè's couch. My phone says it's almost noon—I've slept eight hours with the help of two Trazodone and a beer.

Noè sticks his head into the room to find me awake, staring at the ceiling.

"Good morning, girl."

"Mornin'." My throat is raw, and my voice comes out in a croak.

"We have an appointment at one thirty," he says, and I nod. Today, we take care of the business end of our son's death. Late last night by the fire pit, we agreed on a memorial service that celebrates Joshua's life instead of focusing on his death. And that Joshua should be cremated. And that this all should happen posthaste.

I make my way to the bathroom. The woman in the mirror is a stranger. Everything about me has changed. The lines on my face. The bones in my wrists. There's no part of me that is the same as it was two days ago. I am older and less alive. I'm a slipshod version of myself in yesterday's clothes. Brushing my teeth is the most I can manage, but I imagine the mortician has experience with grieving mothers and our tangled hair and stained T-shirts.

. . .

Bill drives us to Family Funeral Care—he and I in the front seat, Noè and his brother Isael in the back. A woman in a business suit greets us with a quiet smile. She shows us to a room with a long lacquered cherrywood table holding catalogues of caskets, urns, and other things no one wants to buy. I pour coffee for Bill and hot water for Noè, and we wait for someone to tell us what to do next.

The funeral director, Mr. Alvarez, is a bald man of about sixty with a potbelly and glasses too big for his face. Noè shakes his hand and introduces us all. Tells Mr. Alvarez we need to make arrangements for our son. We want a cremation. A memorial service. Mr. Alvarez answers, and, even though he talks slowly and repeats himself often, his words sound odd and confusing. Why are we here? Why is this man talking about my son?

"So if you'd like, we can go get him now." His words pull me out of my head and back into the room.

I hate thinking about Joshua being at the morgue. The top priority is to get him out of there. "Yes," I say.

Noè nods in agreement. "As soon as possible."

Mr. Alvarez opens a catalogue and asks, "What are you thinking about urns?"

As Noè looks through the pages of the catalogue, I realize that there is no part of me that is interested in picking out an urn for my son. The thought is obscene. Offensive. It makes bile come up in my throat.

I'm grateful this is something Noè feels equipped to do.

"I want to put his picture on the front," he says, "in a frame, you know?" He turns the catalogue to me and points to a rectangular, sand-colored marble version.

"It's good. Whatever you want is fine with me."

Noè feels a connection to the ashes I do not feel. He wants to keep them all together, in one place, so he can touch them, talk to them, pray over them.

"I can keep him for a while, and then you can take him to Michigan for a while," Noè says. "Like joint custody." We all laugh a little.

"You keep it," I tell him. I don't want the urn at my house. I wouldn't be able to stand the daily reminder of what I've lost. My son is gone. The ashes are just what is left of the package he came in.

Noè has questions. How long will the cremation take? How can the funeral home be sure they get all his ashes? Mr. Alvarez answers in a steady voice while Noè nods his head.

"How old are they?" I ask. Blank looks from the others tell me I'm the only one still thinking about our earlier conversation.

"The people who will go get him from the morgue. How old are they?"

Alvarez seems puzzled. I imagine he's trying to figure out what answer to my question will make me feel better rather than worse. "They are . . . um . . . both very professional. There's a man around fifty and a woman in her twenties," he says. "Can I ask what your concern is?"

I think for a moment about my children. Claudia has not yet settled on an identity that feels right, but Kimberly and Joshua both identify as the races of their fathers. They are brown people, unlike their mother. Once in a grocery store line a stranger making conversation asked me how long I'd had them. I stammered in response to his question, then wrote him off as a weirdo, before I realized he thought my children were adopted.

Now, my son's body—brown and tattooed—is lying at the city morgue. Are people touching him? Talking about him? When they look at him, do they think "gangbanger?" Will some kid with purple pimples say, "Hey, did you hear the one about the Mexican who went to heaven?"

I've spent my life helping my children define their own identities and be empowered by them. Teaching them to embrace all of who they are and be proud. And they have learned the lesson well. The thought of Joshua facing an indignity in his death is too painful to take.

"I know that this is their job . . ." My voice seems to be coming from the ceiling rather than anywhere in my body. "And they do this every day . . ." How can I tell him how special this person is? That loading him in a hearse and driving him across town should be an act of reverence. Done with compassion and dignity.

Mr. Alvarez presses his lips together and nods his understanding. "I will go."

I exhale. "Treat him like he's yours," I say, and he answers he will.

"Services for young people usually draw a large crowd," Mr. Alvarez tells us. "If you are ready to move forward, the main chapel is available on Sunday at two p.m." We agree, sign the papers, and shake hands with Mr. Alvarez.

"If you want to see Joshua," he adds as we are getting ready to leave. Noè turns to look at him, but not me. A blank stare into the hallway keeps me from acknowledging this vile thing he has said. "You can visit him at noon tomorrow. Before the cremation process starts."

.   .   .

Noè married his second wife, Michele, when Josh was three. I was eaten alive with jealousy. She was refined, in my mind, and had everything I did not. A college graduate, a beautiful woman, and kind on top of it. The first time I met her, I had gone to Noè's apartment to pick up Joshua's car seat. There was no answer when I knocked and the lights were out, so I let myself into his apartment with a key he had given me once when he went out of town. Instead of an empty apartment, I found Noè and Michele lying on a pallet on the floor watching television. At that moment, I knew our relationship had changed. No more keys to each other's apartment. No more opening the refrigerator to find something to munch on at the other person's house. He was in love and intended to make a life with the woman lying next to him on that pallet.

"Michele washed the cover," he said and handed me the car seat. Stammering, I'm sure, I thanked her and let myself out.

Over the years, we all matured and made a silent commitment to put our son before ourselves. It wasn't always easy, as we couldn't have been more different. Michele came from a loving family in Arkansas, taught elementary school, kept a beautiful house, and warmed her husband's towels in the dryer while he was in the tub. I was a single mom bumbling my way through life in a way that left everyone involved battered and bruised. The only thing we had in common at first was a cheerful, sensitive little boy who captured our hearts, but that was enough to keep us focused on what was important. When we both had more children, Joshua proclaimed that he would be known to his sisters only as Bubba, and there was no reason to use terms like "half" or "step" when talking about them. Stepsisters were those people you met after your parents had divorced and married someone who already had children. Sisters, well, sisters were those people you bathed with, suffered through chicken pox with, and argued over the last cookie with.

"Family is family," Joshua said. So Michele and I became two ends of the same chain, with Joshua as the connecting link. Indeed, we became family.

5

I wake up on the couch again, earlier than the day before. Noè
has pulled a futon mattress into the living room, and Bill is sleeping there, wrapped in blankets to shield him from the arctic-level
air-conditioning that's already working hard. I listen to voices
coming from the kitchen, not able to tell who is talking. There are
sobs. Whispers. Claudia is sleeping opposite me on the sectional.
One arm is thrown over her head so her hand touches me—a
tentative offering of connection from a child who is fighting back
her own sadness to support me in mine.

None of my children could say they had an easy childhood,
and Claudia has dealt with more than her share of turmoil.
Though I was thirty-one when I had her and had a full-time job
helping newly immigrated refugees settle in the United States, my
choice of partners still left much to be desired. Claudia's father,
Ramon, was a Cuban immigrant who worked doing repair welding on marine vessels on the Mississippi River. He was introduced
to methamphetamines by his coworkers to help manage the long
hours and quick turnaround time required when United States
Coast Guard ships came into dock needing repair. After many
days of working nonstop without sleep or food—and usually after

he was in debt to the drug dealer for more than his weekly paycheck—he would come home exhausted and crashing from his days-long high. It was then he became violent.

By day, I talked to people who had fled their countries to escape war and political or religious persecution. I often took Joshua, then five, with me on home visits if the family had children. More than once, we introduced families to American phenomena like thirty-one flavors of ice cream and Chuck E. Cheese's. Joshua was a natural at building bridges, and children's laughter crossed any cultural barriers that existed.

But by night, Joshua lived in an environment where his mother was beaten, spit on, and subjected to every other humiliating act imaginable. Many times, I would go in his room and crawl into the bottom bunk with Joshua afterward and hold him while we both cried. There were times I thought I would die. There were even times I wished I would. From inside the relationship, I couldn't see a way out of the hell I was living, and death seemed like the only way out.

One night, in early 1997, my seven-year-old son came into the living room to find me being held by the hair. With fire in his eyes and his jaw set, he put his finger on the red button marked "Emergency" on our house alarm and said one word.

"Ramon."

Joshua looked defiantly into the face of a raging grown man intending to do whatever was necessary to stop his mother from being hurt. Joshua's actions ended the attack, but I realized then it was only a matter of time before Ramon would hit my son. I had to leave and do it quickly.

I had already left Ramon when I found out I was pregnant with Claudia. Ramon didn't like living without us. He sat in his car outside my apartment for long hours watching who came and went. He broke in to my car in the parking lot of my job and left it ransacked. Once at the dinner table, Joshua reported that he'd seen Ramon leaning against a tree on the playground at his school. I tried to maintain a sense of safety for the kids, but I lived in fear for my life. I had an order of protection and called the police every time something happened, but they always seemed to arrive just after he had fled. The day he was finally arrested, Claudia was a year old. She had been hospitalized for a couple of days with a high fever and a rash that looked like tiny blood vessels had burst all over her face. The night we arrived at the hospital, the pediatrician on staff let me know that Claudia's condition was serious and that I should be prepared for the worst.

"She could get very sick very quickly," the doctor said. So I called Ramon.

After a few days, the fever and rash both disappeared, and we were released to go home. Later that day, he came to my apartment assuming he was now welcome. When I told him he was not, he attacked me. Claudia was in my arms, and, by the time it was over, she had a bloody nose.

When the police arrived, I let them know that I was done. My nerves and my patience had run out.

"You can either follow me to his house and arrest him or follow me to his house and arrest me, because I'm going to kill him," I said. For so many years, I couldn't imagine a way out of the relationship that didn't involve one of us dying. I decided it was not going to be me.

One of the police officers who responded was a woman who had been to my house many times. She saw something in me now that let her know I was on the edge. That day, the police followed me across town in three squad cars and arrested Ramon. Afterward, I rolled down the windows, turned up the radio, and went to pick up Joshua from school with Claudia strapped into her car seat babbling along with the music.

Three years later, when Ramon got out of jail, he seemed to have good intentions of living a better life. He got his job back at the marine company and paid child support. He married a woman with a son a little older than Claudia. But karma is, as they say, a bitch. A month after his wedding, he fell fifteen feet onto a concrete dry dock and became paralyzed from the armpits down.

For some people, tragedy is a catalyst for doing self-inventory and growing from the experience. But if Ramon was an angry and violent person before his accident, he became an angrier and more violent person afterward. The only difference was that he was in a wheelchair. His relationship with Claudia was troubled. After many weekend visits where she witnessed violent fights between him and his wife, I moved to have their visits supervised. Claudia and I established a safe word, the secret word that would immediately end the visit if she was feeling uncomfortable. After a couple of uses of the safe word, visits dwindled to birthdays and holidays. After I married Bill and moved to Michigan, contact with Ramon all but stopped. He had fallen right back into the world of drinking and drugging in spite of his physical challenges.

. . .

Claudia has asked for her father, but I am torn. Would Joshua have wanted Ramon to be there? Ramon was physically and emotionally abusive to me, and Joshua never forgot what it was like to live in the house where he was in fear of a person who was supposed to love and protect him. Now, on this couch watching my daughter sleep, I imagine all I can do is support her. She has lost her big brother, another hurt I cannot heal. I put my hand over hers, and, closing my eyes, I etch the feel of my daughter's touch into my memory.

Soon, I leave the couch and move to sit in the kitchen. Then, I sit on the patio. Sitting seems to be all I can muster with despair weighing on me like the black wool funeral dress that lies wadded in my duffel bag. I finish a cup of coffee before realizing there is no sugar or milk in it.

Noè joins me on the patio, still wearing pajama pants with cartoon characters. "I'm gonna go see my boy," he says.

He needs to see his son again, touch his face. Kiss him. Tell him not to worry about his sisters. But I push the thought as far away as I can. I don't want to go. When people ask, "You don't want to see your son?" I answer with a violent, "No!"

I'm afraid of everything—that he won't look like himself. That he will. That I'll never get the image out of my head. I search and search for a part of me that wants to see him, but I know that the image of my son's lifeless body will haunt me for the rest of my life. Not going is selfish and an act of self-preservation at the same time.

. . .

Much to Joshua's annoyance, Noè maintained his friendship with Ramon after my relationship with Ramon had ended. Recognizing how much Ramon's life sucked, Noè helped him with things like changing lightbulbs and raking leaves. Noè believed that Ramon had paid his dues and deserved some slack. Joshua did not. Over the years, Joshua and I talked many times about the years we lived with Ramon. I hoped that Joshua would find compassion for Ramon and give himself the gift of forgiveness. Comparing Ramon and me, I came out of my relationship with Ramon as a stronger person. The same cannot be said for Ramon.

Noè knows where to find Ramon, so we drive to Jackson Avenue where a stretch of convenience stores and taquerias mark the western border of Little Mexico. Ramon is just where Noè predicted he would be, sitting in his wheelchair beside a building, a pint of vodka stuffed down the front of his vinyl running pants.

"Spot me," I say as I get out of the car and walk toward a group of men leaning against a building. When Ramon sees me, he avoids making eye contact for a moment, then wheels toward me.

When I tell him Joshua has died, he wails. Pulls his hair and pounds on his chest and yells, "Why not me?"

I have to admit to myself, I had the same thought.

6

When Bill and I met in 2004, he let me know he was on his way back to Michigan. Ten years earlier, he'd moved to Memphis to marry his first wife, but it had never felt like home to him. I told him I could relate. Even though I'd lived in Memphis my whole life, it held nothing but pain for me. It was all unbearable, and I told Bill I would be on a bullet train out of Memphis myself if I ever got the chance.

Bill had decided during his first marriage that he did not want to father children and had taken steps to ensure it. There was a certain irony to our immediate connection, since I was by then parenting four kids on my own—Kimberly had come back to live with me when she was fourteen, and I had gotten custody of my niece, Alicia, because my sister was struggling with a crack cocaine addiction.

A year and a half after we met, when I was thirty-eight, Joshua walked me down the aisle to where my girls and Bill waited. In a chapel with stained glass and hardwood floors, a fiddle, a banjo, and an acoustic guitar played. Joshua, sixteen, wore his first tuxedo, danced with his sisters, and sneaked champagne. I cried that day just before the chapel doors opened for me to enter the room.

Joshua crooked out his arm for me to take. With his father's looks and charm, Joshua had more than his share of interest from the girls at his high school. With tears welling up in my eyes, I told my sweet, handsome son I hoped he would someday find a partner who made him feel the way I felt with Bill.

I've often said the only reason I gave Joshua a choice about whether to move to Michigan or stay in Memphis with his father was because I was *sure* he would come with me. We had always been so close, and, even though I had no idea what life in another city would be like, I was excited to get my kids away from Memphis and into what I believed would be a better life. When Joshua told me he wasn't coming with us, I buried my head in my pillow and cried.

"I've been with you all these years, Mama. I think I should spend some time with Dad."

My heart broke. Kimberly was grown and out exploring the world. She had moved to Dallas for a short time, then to North Carolina. I had come to terms with not living in the same city she did. But Joshua was still a teenager. The next couple of years would be huge for him as he figured out how he was going to walk through the world as a man, and I wanted to be a part of it. Still, leaving Memphis felt like an opportunity for me to be free of the pain of my past and that—along with a supportive partner and a healthy relationship—gave me hope I might come to know myself better. Become more of who I was meant to be or at least less of the broken person I had been.

Three months after our wedding, Bill, Claudia, Alicia, and I packed everything we owned and headed north.

We landed in a funky little college town in southeast Michigan, where we bought a huge 1922 Craftsman house. The previous owner restored the floors and other woodwork, and it had nineteen windows just on the first floor. Having a university right in town and another one town over gave us access to a wide diversity of cultures and all the food and music that came with it. I walked the girls to school and often found the principal playing basketball with the kids on the blacktop in the mornings. But I felt like a mama duck always looking behind me to count ducklings, and I was always one short. Josh spent the summers with us, and, at the end of the summer when I put him on the bus to go home, my heart broke.

We'd picked the town we lived in because it had so many of the things we valued. We'd picked the house because we were newlyweds and thought we had the world by the throat. But time proved that I'd made another bad decision that would end up hurting my children.

At the onset of puberty, Alicia began a cycle of behavior destructive to herself and everyone around her: self-harm, destruction of property (mostly mine), drug use, sexual acting out. The time and energy required to help her work through this caustic combination of adolescence and abandonment issues were more than I could handle while working full-time. I left my job with a regional health system so I could be home more while still bringing in a little money to help toward the house. A few months into my self-employment, Bill was downsized from his corporate IT job. Stress was high in the household, and, to top it off, we had a three-hundred-thousand-dollar mortgage to contend with.

I was so tired of struggling to pay our bills. As lovely as it was, we were slaves to our house. Moving to Michigan was supposed to change things for the better, but it turned out to be more of the same. Was it me? Was I missing some big life lesson that could only be learned through struggle? Or was I just never meant to exhale at all?

Together, Bill and I made a change. We were both weary of what we called the hamster wheel and wanted a simpler life. A life where we worked to live and not the other way around. A life that spoke our values louder than we ourselves could. We let the bank know to proceed with foreclosure and filed bankruptcy on the thousands of dollars in medical bills we had racked up while trying to help Alicia stabilize. Bill enrolled in the Organic Farmer Training Program at Michigan State University, and we rented a small farmhouse ten miles from Ypsilanti. The next summer when Joshua came to Michigan, he helped Bill to start our family farm. For hours every day, he worked side by side with Bill to plant, weed, and harvest food to feed our family and a dozen more. He was a hard worker and a born salesman, talking to people in the grocery store about the benefits of eating organic. He even declared that once he got back to Dad's, "We're getting chickens!"

In those months, I felt like I was getting a glimpse of the man Joshua was becoming. I also got a glimpse of how rewarding it can be to cook a good meal for hungry folks at the end of a long day. Especially when the food was grown by the hands of people you love.

7

If my life has taught me nothing else, it has taught me that every lovely moment you have, there will be despicable moments in equal and opposite measure to balance things out. Because of this, there were times when I didn't know what to do with the love I had for my children. It felt overwhelming. Like it might overtake me. Maybe even make me go crazy like my mama had. Needing someone too much was a guarantee that they would go away, and I worried that one day my children would be taken away from me with one flip of a cosmic switch. So I prepared myself. I imagined what it would feel like. How I would act. I planned my response. In my mind, I would be graceful. Even enlightened about it. But there is no grace in me.

. . .

I have seen death before. I've even been in the room with it. Looked it in the eye and kept right on moving. One year before Joshua died—almost to the date—Kimberly and I drove through Kentucky to the Cumberland Plateau. My twenty-seven-year-old cousin, Sherrie, had overdosed on heroin in a cheap hotel in

Crossville, Tennessee, and her mother had agreed to wait until Kimberly could get there to take her off life support. Kimberly was less than a year older than Sherrie, and they had been sister-cousins as children. There are pictures of them in diapers playing in a sprinkler in my grandparents' backyard, Kimberly's creamy brown skin and dark hair and eyes contrasting with Sherrie's milk-white skin, blond hair, and blue eyes. I secretly thought of them as "Night and Day"—secretly, because such a blatant reference to Kimberly's race would have been perceived as an attempt to draw attention to something my family tried hard to ignore.

My Uncle Bud, Mama's brother, was Sherrie's father. I remember him telling me when she was born that you couldn't parent and be on dope at the same time, so he was quitting IV drugs. In the end, though, he was only able to trade drugs for alcohol, and his relationship with his daughter suffered. As they got older, Kimberly and Sherrie grew apart. Sherrie isolated herself more and more as drugs and alcohol played a bigger part in her life. Even though they hadn't talked in years, Kimberly wanted to say good-bye.

We stood at the foot of the bed as the respiratory therapist talked sweetly to Sherrie and removed her breathing tube. Sherrie's lips turned blue, and the beeps and lines on the monitor slowed almost immediately. As I saw it, my job was to support Kimberly and, to some extent, Sherrie's mother. Having my own feelings would get in the way of that, so I watched like an outsider rather than a full participant in the tragedy of her death. I went to the nurse's station and got a stethoscope when her mother said, "I wish I could hear her heart." When her mother pressed "Play" on the gospel tape she'd brought, I opened the blinds to the sunny April day, and we sang as Sherrie slipped out the window, made her way through the trees, kissed the mountaintops, and floated out into the great beyond.

Later that year, Joshua, Claudia, and I went to the funeral of the man who raised me—my grandfather. Before he was diagnosed with Alzheimer's, we talked on the phone often, catching up on his latest plans for travel, his health, and what was happening at the Baptist church he and his wife attended. Often, he would tell stories about his younger days, something I was always interested in hearing more about. We compared memories from my childhood, and, often, his perspective helped me understand things differently from the way I remembered. It is not an exaggeration to say he was the only man who had ever been a constant in my life. Over the years, he and Mamaw were my parents when my own parents couldn't be.

My parents had not married—a point that offended my grandfather to the depths of his soul. Before my father met Mama, he came home from Vietnam with his own psychiatric problems, and so my grandfather refused any attempt my father ever made at seeing us. Though they never had legal custody of me and my sister, our maternal grandparents were our only touch point of sanity through a childhood filled with chaos. Knowing that one day his Alzheimer's would put a stranger in my grandfather's place, a person absent of the history we shared, made me sad. Seeing him confused and afraid would have devastated me. In the years after his diagnosis, I made sure to say all the things I wanted to say to him and made peace with his imminent departure. Once he was in a nursing home, I didn't visit anymore.

On one of my visits early in his illness, he said, "I want to show you something," and drove me to his family cemetery in Beech Bluff, Tennessee. My paternal great-great-grandfather had owned the land where the cemetery is located. The story goes that he sold the land to the town of Beech Bluff to build its first schoolhouse. The school still exists today, with the cemetery tucked behind it down a winding dirt road.

When we got there, my grandfather pointed out a single head-stone already engraved with his name and date of birth. Bettye, the woman he married after my grandmother died, was to be buried in another cemetery beside her first husband, the father of her children. Since my grandmother had been cremated, he had decided to be buried here, alongside his mother and father, his grandparents, and several members of the family whose stones in this graveyard were now chipped and mossy, their names barely decipherable.

In spite of the gravestone, the family had my grandfather cremated. After the service in the parlor of what was once a plantation house, I told the kids I wanted to put flowers at the gravestone in Beech Bluff in honor of my conversation with him. It was late in the day, and my GPS signal was confused by the twists and turns and changing names of the old country roads. By the time we found the cemetery, night was upon us. A white horse galloped in circles in a pasture beside the cemetery as we carefully stepped around graves that were hundreds of years old, finally finding the right one.

In that cemetery, in the dark, six months before he died, my son and I talked about what we wanted to happen after our own deaths.

"Do they have to put all that makeup on you?" he asked. The body lying in the casket at the viewing hardly looked like my grandfather at all.

"No," I told him. "Your family is in charge of your funeral. As long as they know your wishes, you can have it however you want it."

We stood together and listened to the horse gallop around the pasture while Claudia examined gravestones nearby.

"I don't want to be closed in a box," he said. "I want to be cremated."

"Me too," I agreed, then added, "I hope I'm not around when your time comes, but, if I am, I will make sure it happens the way you want it."

8

It's Saturday afternoon and Michele stands at the stove and absently stirs a pot of something. I slide into a chair at the kitchen bar.

"What's this?" I ask, picking up a manila envelope with Joshua's name written on the front in black marker.

"It's the police report," Michele tells me. "They gave it to Noè at the morgue."

I turn it over in my hands. "Are there pictures?"

"No." She puts a lid on the pot. "Just details from the accident."

The police report is a diagram of a road. A trajectory of dotted lines going over a set of railroad tracks. There's an apartment complex on one side of the road. On the other side—the side where the accident occurred—is an open field with a lone utility pole between it and the street. A stick figure body and a motorcycle are drawn in just below it.

The narrative identifies Joshua as a twenty-three-year-old Hispanic male heading north on Raleigh Lagrange Road on a Harley-Davidson motorcycle.

Underneath "Cause of Accident" is written the word "racing," underlined twice.

Racing. The word makes my brain explode. I'm angry at Josh. Angry at whomever he was racing with. Angry at the police officer for writing the word so smugly, so definitively, as if to suggest there is no doubt that the blame for Joshua's death lies squarely on his own shoulders.

Joshua's motorcycle is not a racing bike. It's a cruiser with a distressed brown leather saddle and matching leather saddlebags. What he loved most about riding was the freedom that came from it and the camaraderie with others who owned Harley-Davidsons. Could someone have challenged him at a red light, revving their engine and giving him a taunting look that made him hell-bent on leaving them in the dust? It's possible, I decide. There's no predicting what a twenty-three-year-old will do when he feels that his manhood is on the line.

· · ·

That goddamned motorcycle. A year and a half before Joshua's accident, I received a text message with a picture of it. It was a beautiful bike, but the thought of someone I loved being on it worried me.

"Nice!" I replied. "You gonna buy it?"

"I just did!" Joshua answered.

Pictures continued over the next couple of days, and I tried to focus on the positive energy coming from him instead of the possible dangers. Later that week, I got a call from him.

"Ma, I have a problem." I could tell by the tone of his voice that his use of the word "problem" was really his way of saying, "I'm about to tell you something you might not be okay with."

Turned out that while he was at Bumpus Harley-Davidson of Memphis buying his motorcycle, he'd asked whether they were hiring and then filled out an application to work in the maintenance shop. They had called him back and sent him for a drug test and were now offering him a position. That was how he rolled. So charming and charismatic he could walk into a place of business, make a purchase, and walk out with a job offer.

"The problem is," he said, "I've already committed to work on the farm this summer. I wouldn't be able to do that if I took this job."

Which was, of course, not a problem at all. When I told Bill about the conversation, he said, "Hell, if he doesn't take the job, I will." Unlike me, Bill has a history of riders in his family. In fact, his Uncle Vern died on his Harley in a freak accident much like Joshua's.

Josh was promoted twice in the year he worked for Bumpus. I got regular updates from Josh about work and the people there. He was learning a lot, he said, from the men in the shop. With classic rock playing in the background, they told stories while they worked. They were, according to Joshua, "old biker dudes. All tattooed up. Sometimes they're assholes, but really good guys."

. . .

"No black at the funeral," Noè declares. "Joshua wouldn't want everyone to be all sad and dressed in black." When it's suggested that we all wear Harley T-shirts, blue jeans, and one of Joshua's bandanas in our hair, it feels right. Michele and I will wear matching T-shirts, and I head out to buy them.

The Cinco de Mayo celebration at Bumpus Harley-Davidson is in full swing when I arrive. Hundreds of shiny motorcycles are in the parking lot, and music is playing loudly. People from every walk of life are talking and laughing. I understand why Joshua liked it here.

"Honey." A woman approaches me with arms stretched wide for a hug. The past few days have been such a haze, I'm not sure if I've met her before. But I'll take all the hugs I can get.

"Listen, if you're comfortable with it, the guy on the other bike is here. He'd like to talk to you."

"The other bike?" I ask.

"The other bike that was on Raleigh Lagrange when Josh wrecked."

Not knowing whether I will regret it, I say yes. He is, after all, the last person to see my son alive. The woman says she'll tell him, and I make a beeline for the T-shirt rack. I'm already feeling conspicuous and out of place. Like an alien who landed on a planet of people whose children are alive.

I'm sifting through shirts when I notice a bearded young man standing off to my side. I look up and make eye contact with him.

"Are you the guy?" I ask.

He says he is, introduces himself as Blasco, and hugs me. There's a woman in nurse scrubs standing behind him with her hand on his arm. There's polite conversation, and then he says, "I thought you might like to know what happened. I saw everything."

The room closes in on me. Is there enough air in this room for all these people?

"The police report says you guys were racing," I say.

"No, ma'am. We were not racing," he tells me. "Maybe they thought we were because there we were, two young men on motorcycles. But that's not what happened."

It was just after three o'clock on a Wednesday afternoon. Blasco had just gotten off from work and was waiting at a stop sign when Joshua crossed the road, passing in front of him. When he passed, Joshua greeted him with the traditional biker wave.

"I remember thinking this is one cool cat," Blasco tells me. Harley riders and sport bike riders are not known for acknowledging one another's existence, he says.

As he came up to the railroad tracks, Joshua took his left hand off his handlebars and reached behind to one of his saddlebags. The railroad tracks didn't run exactly perpendicular. Instead, they crossed the road at just the right angle to grab the front tire of the motorcycle. With only one hand on the handlebars, Joshua wrestled for control of the bike until he was thrown headfirst into that lone utility pole in front of the open field.

Blasco stopped his bike and went to Joshua.

"His wallet flew out of his jeans and was lying in the street, and I opened it to find out his name," Blasco tells me. "I said, 'Joshua. Stay with me, brother.' But I could tell he was already gone." Blasco's head drops. "There was nothing I could do but stay with him and pray until the ambulance got there."

. . .

Back at Noè's house, I sit staring out the window when Noè and Bill come through the kitchen door. "He looks good," Noè says when he comes through the door with Bill following behind him. "Looks like he's just sleeping."

I don't believe him. Noè is a person who cannot stand to see people he cares about in pain. To say something himself that will cause pain is unimaginable. He'll do his best to absorb all the pain himself if it means he can spare the people he loves. But the bike was practically untouched as well. When Noè retrieved it from the impound lot, there was only a scratch on the gas tank and one on the tailpipe. Noè was able to crank it up and ride it right off the lot. Nothing about this makes sense. How can my son be dead yet have no visible injuries? How could he have hit the only utility pole in the area? And how could he have hit it headfirst?

Bill accompanied Noè to the funeral home for two reasons. If Noè had found himself unable to go into the viewing room, Bill would have gone instead and reported back. Second, Kimberly was going, and Bill wanted to be there to support her when she saw her brother. He comes in behind Noè and joins the conversation.

"There was a little blood in his ear, but otherwise he looked just like himself," Bill adds.

I hope with everything I have that whatever the cause of death, it was quick. That Joshua didn't suffer. That he wasn't afraid or in pain. I'm grateful that we didn't have to see him lying helpless in a hospital bed or decide when to take him off life support.

Make no mistake, whatever caused it, the result is that my son is dead. But at least it seems his death was merciful.

Later that day, I sit on the patio searching for a piece of myself that can put my son's life into words. So that notification of tomorrow's service will happen in time, the funeral home needs the obituary by four, and I've waited until the last possible minute to put pen to paper.

I confer with Michele, then write the names of people who were once my in-laws, carefully spelling the names of Joshua's aunts, uncles, and cousins. Some of the names I write are the same people who are now bringing me coffee and crying with me. Reminding me we are still and will always be family. *Somos familia.*

I write the names of each of Joshua's sisters—between me and his father, there are five. I consider the order and list them by age: Kimberly, Kelsi, Alicia, Claudia, and Bella Rose. Joshua had his sisters' names tattooed on his right bicep, his promise to always hold them in his protection.

My thoughts turn to my son. Who was this person named Joshua? He was handsome. Strikingly so. The kind of handsome that made people stop and stare. And he was charming. Every person who met him felt like they had just met their best friend. He was loyal, sometimes to a fault, and no friend or family member could ever do wrong in his eyes. He saw the good in everybody. But he never shied away from a fight, especially if he was standing up for someone who couldn't stand up for themselves.

He had goals and dreams, though, like his mother, focusing on only one thing quickly became intolerable. He wrote poetry and lyrics. He played soccer and lacrosse and practiced mixed martial arts. He loved working with his hands and considered becoming a welder like his father. Watching him figure out his life was a mixed bag of excitement and stark terror for me.

Joshua began talking about joining the military at the end of high school, around the same time I started to hear rumblings that the United States might reinstate a draft to relieve the troops who had already done far more than their fair share in the Iraq and Afghanistan Wars. When I asked what it was about military service that appealed to him, he said the physical aspect of it. And, he said, he wanted to do important work.

"Your dad was in the military, wasn't he?" he asked me one day.

"Marines. Fought in Vietnam."

"And your grandfather was too."

"Army. Fought in World War II."

"Ma. It's like a tradition."

Josh had a point. The two men who had most influenced my life—one by his presence and the other by his absence—were both wartime veterans.

Still, I couldn't stomach the idea. With all his drive and charisma, and the fact that there were two active wars, Joshua would undoubtedly end up on the front lines. In fact, he would insist on being there. And even if he didn't die in battle, what would become of his spirit? Being a soldier means being able to accept that there are some humans whom the world would be better off without.

I called Noè to talk strategy about how to get this crazy idea out of Joshua's head, and we devised a plan. He couldn't enlist until he was eighteen anyway. Between now and then, we would take every opportunity to point out the drawbacks of military service. And if a draft came to pass? We'd send him to Mexico to live with Noè's sister and finish high school.

Both Noè and I were intent on Joshua going to college, and we proudly moved him in to his dorm at Middle Tennessee State University. In his first semester, he enrolled in JROTC and talked seriously about being commissioned as an officer when he finished college. When he shared pictures of himself in that uniform, I could not deny that he looked like a natural. In the end, I had to tell him he had my blessing. And if he died fighting for something he believed in, I would be proud to say he was my son.

Going away to college gave Josh an opportunity for independence he hadn't had before. He was highly intelligent and a critical thinker, but he also needed to be around other people to feel balanced. Like many college freshmen, he partied too much and studied too little. At a party during his freshman year, an argument with his girlfriend turned violent when she caught him dancing with another girl. Witnesses reported that she jumped on his back and pounded him right there on the dance floor. Later that night, Joshua went to her apartment and found her there with another guy. Chaos ensued. By morning, Joshua had a domestic violence charge, which ultimately kept him from being able to join the military. I'm not sure whether to count that as unfortunate or not. Spending a couple of days in a jail cell in Murfreesboro, Tennessee, was a good lesson for Joshua. Perhaps it even kept him alive a little longer than if he had joined the military.

And passing the last few days with his friends and family, I've learned things about my son I never knew. Like how he was the person they went to for advice. How he encouraged his friends to follow their dreams and their hearts. And, even though I knew he had a tattoo on his right shoulder that read "Cry Here," I didn't realize how often he offered that shoulder to others. I guess Joshua did a fine job of figuring out who he was, and my pompous worries of him flailing without me in the same city was my way of pumping up my self-importance.

. . .

When he bought it, Noë's house was tucked into a forest. Deer grazed in his yard. Joshua and his friends spent hours on adventures in these woods, climbing trees, and more than once he came home with injuries. Fifteen years later, the city has sprawled out to meet the forest. Subdivisions with neat little houses all the same shape and size on three sides. But the patio, where I sit now, is secluded, surrounded by trees and bushes and is peaceful save for the booming bass of passing cars on the street below.

Right outside my vision, just above the red azalea bush, something moves. Then, a buzz, close enough for me to feel the wind it generates on my cheek. A ruby-throated hummingbird hangs in the air ten inches from my face. Flitting. A flash of movement, color, and light. One moment here, the next moment gone, just like my son. For an instant, we see one another. Soul to soul. And for that moment, I remember joy.

9

The obituary is sent, and I go sit under a tree at the back of Noé's yard. My sister, Jessica, and Alicia arrive. After Michele points to me across the yard, Alicia joins Joshua's other sisters by the tree house, and Jessica joins me under the tree. The tears have stopped, but the pain still hovers in my chest, threatening to erupt. The tears return when I see her, and we sit together on the ground and cry for a while. It's a different feeling being on this end of sisterly support. I am the proverbial older sister—quick to the rescue.

"Did you tell Mama?" I ask her.

Jessica and I have an understanding. I raised her daughter for twelve years while she battled a crack cocaine addiction. Now that she is clean, she gets to deal with our mother. Even on my best days, I struggle to find compassion for Mama. In my mind, she chose dope over me. In fact, I moved seven hundred miles away to avoid ever having to hold a conversation with her. And I like it that way.

"Yeah, I just left her house. I'm not sure how well she gets it yet."

Does that mean she was in denial or out of her head on opiates? I decide not to ask.

The first time I cried at my wedding was when my son took my arm just before walking me down the aisle. The second time was when I realized that, aside from my children, my grandfather was the only member of my family in attendance. I had sent Mama an invitation, unsure of whether I wanted her there or not. Her being there and causing a scene would have been terrible. Not coming at all was worse. I feel the same about Joshua's funeral.

At my grandfather's funeral six months ago, she nodded asleep in the front row while I stood at the podium and talked about the man I respected most in the world. Before that, she missed my cousin's funeral altogether, even though Sherrie was her only niece. I have been hurt by her selfishness so many times in my life I flinch to even hear her name. Every time I let myself have hope that things might be different, something rips off the scab.

And yet . . .

I want more for her than what she has chosen. I want her to have a *real* life—one where she gets out of bed and offers something to the world. I want my children to have a relationship with their grandmother. And I want a relationship with my mother that doesn't hurt.

"I need you to tell her that if she can't do it . . ."

Did I mean what I was about to say?

"If she can't come to the funeral without taking something first, she should just stay home. Under no circumstances can she come to my son's funeral fucked up."

Jessica looks down, picking blades of grass and arranging them on her knee. "I can do that," she says and nods. I'm glad to have a protector of my own.

.   .   .

Explaining my relationship with my mother requires more insight than I possess. As long as I can remember, my relationship with her has caused me pain and confusion. Anyone who has spent time with an addict understands the addict's way of making you doubt your own perception of reality. Mama is the same. For her own survival, she crafts a version of reality that isn't as painful for her, and she holds on to it for dear life. No amount of proof will get her to admit the truth. If she says the sky is green, looking up changes nothing. Tough shit for those who don't live inside her head.

And it's not always big, important things like whether one of her friends had crept into bed with you when you were eight or if you hadn't eaten for two days. One year, as an act of goodwill, I made her favorite Mexican dish for her birthday: pozole complete with lemon, chopped onion, and cabbage. The kids and I took it to her house already warmed, and we ate and laughed and had a good time.

A few days later, I called and asked, "Have you finished the soup? I need my pot back."

"That's my soup pot," she said. Aw hell. Here we go.

"Ma, I left that pot there on your birthday when I made pozole. Remember?"

She gave me the most detailed explanation: where she bought it, how much she paid for it, what the weather was like that day. I argued for a while but quickly gave up. After all, the soup pot was in her possession, and everyone knows that possession is nine-tenths of the law!

The next Christmas, the old hag gave me a soup pot.

For a child, these invented realities were crazy-making. Because of these experiences, lying to my children is unbearable. We never did Santa, the Tooth Fairy, or any of those other myth-ical creatures that sneak into your home at night. There were no cutesy names for genitalia or body functions. My goal, though not conscious and articulated, was to validate in the clearest possible terms what was happening in the world—as much for myself as for my children.

10

Family Funeral Care is a few blocks away from the house my children and I lived in before I met Bill and moved to his house in the suburbs. I bought it a week before Joshua's tenth birthday—my first home, a redbrick bungalow with a Japanese maple in the front yard. The real estate agent told me the neighborhood was full of "newlyweds and nearly deads," which made it a great place for a single mother with three children. We were just a couple of blocks off the main drag for household staples, fast food, and the like. Only a little farther away was the community center where Joshua took karate and went swimming in the summer.

The first week we were there, an elderly neighbor came across the street to greet me. "I'm so glad you bought that house," she said. "I was afraid they were going to sell it to some blacks or Mexicans." I took it as a great opportunity to start things right with my new neighbor, and I assured her she would be seeing lots of both going forward!

We lived there for five years and, despite such an uncertain welcome, built community in a way I had never known. Many summer evenings with parents sitting on porches and children playing across yards, one of us would start to contemplate dinner.

"I've got a pound of hamburger."

"I've got some dry pasta."

Someone else would take off into the house to see if the bagged salad was too wilted, and, before you knew it, we had enough food to feed us all. Since buying a house was something I'd never expected to be able to do, I was sure this was just the start of good things for us.

The days between closing on the house and Josh's birthday were spent painting, since I didn't share the previous owner's fondness for the color of Pepto-Bismol. In a matter of days, the kitchen was sage, my bedroom gray. The plaster walls in Josh's room were dark green with posters of jungle animals hanging over his futon. He was, in his words, practically a teenager and needed a cool room. Kimberly and Claudia shared the other bedroom, which remained perfectly pink at their request.

In many ways, it *was* the start of good things for my little family. Kimberly was finishing high school at Tennessee School for the Deaf, a boarding school outside Nashville, and was excelling both academically and socially. Joshua was in middle school and was playing on the school's soccer team. At two, Claudia was enrolled in a day care on the campus of the University of Memphis in the hands of an amazing and diverse staff.

I was single, living with only my children for the first time in my life. No roommates to scoot my children out of their rooms and into mine. No partner even more broken than I was to control my time and suck away my energy. Three years earlier, I had landed a job answering phone calls from Spanish-speaking employees in a human resources call center, a job I was good at and had managed to hang on to in spite of the chaos with Ramon. To top it all, I was in college and making my way toward a graduate degree. Life felt so different then. So full of possibility.

. . .

Now, as we drive through my old neighborhood toward the funeral home, I feel misty-eyed reminiscing. Summer Avenue runs east and west in this part of town. The bank where I deposited my paycheck each week is here and so is the market where I shopped. On one corner sits Howard's Donuts, where we sometimes stopped for a cruller and chocolate milk on the multi school drop-off. The hotel has been demolished, and, where the bowling alley used to be, a street vendor flops rugs over the top of his custom van and props velvet paintings against the side. Another vendor uses broken concrete blocks like a pedestal to display used toys and cowboy boots.

Things are different from when I left. I have changed, and so has Memphis. Like old lovers, we have grown in different directions.

"Funeral Plans for All Budgets. Se Habla Español."

The words scroll across the electronic billboard outside the funeral home and then blink three times. I chuckle and say, "Isn't that funny?" but no one answers. I wonder whether they will scroll Joshua's name during his service. He would get a kick out of seeing his name in lights. I decide not to ask, conscious of the fact that others aren't always in sync with my sense of humor.

We pull into the parking lot, and I unload the items from the memorial at Noë's house. Bill and Claudia have gone inside and my sister, who is perpetually early, has been waiting for nearly an hour. I hug her quickly and load her up with a poster board with pictures of my blue-eyed baby glued to it.

Across two lanes of traffic, I hear a familiar voice yell, "Fuck you, motherfucker!"

A horn wails, and I turn to see Claudia's dad in his electric wheelchair going full throttle in the fast lane of a four-lane street. A minivan whips around him, causing another car to swerve. Ramon flips them the bird and steers his wheelchair into the funeral home parking lot with the other hand.

"You are crazy." I shake my head at him as he rolls.

"I told Claudia I was comin' and I'm here," he says in heavily accented English, and we hug. No time for resentment today.

"Hardheaded," I mumble and put a stack of photo albums in his lap. "One day you're going to kill yourself in that wheelchair."

"Nah, I not gonna die," he says. "I not gonna die because I *want* to die. The devil told me, suffer, you *hijo de puta*."

The funeral home smells sweet inside. The entryway holds giant paintings of landscapes in gold frames and shiny, dark wood furniture. The people who work here are all dressed in navy-blue suits with pinstriped ties, and they stand with their hands clasped at their waists, smiling warmly as people enter. How many times have they smiled like that? Can they still feel after years of working this job? I nod a hello and walk past them.

The chapel is a rectangular room with rows of pine pews with red cushions along each side. Organ music plays sad and low overhead. I set about arranging, directing, problem solving. I make a sign-up sheet for those who want to speak—one in English and one in Spanish. Where are the translators? We will have people who speak Spanish and people who speak American Sign Language, and I want everyone to be able to feel a part of the service.

"Do something about this music," I tell Bill, and he goes looking for the funeral director with the CD we'd made. After a few minutes, I hear the opening horns of "I Just Can't Wait to Be King" start. *The Lion King* was Joshua's favorite movie, and he knew the words to every song on the sound track. He popped quotes from the movie into conversations and shared inside jokes with his sisters about their favorite scenes. I imagine my son, a grown and tattooed man singing along, and it makes me smile.

And that's when I see my mother. She's wearing a long gauze skirt with flip-flops, and her long, thin hair is pulled back with a barrette. She joins my sister in a seat close to the wall. And from all appearances, she is sober.

11

"I don't know how well I'm going to be able to say these names," the officiant says walking to the podium, "but I'll give it my best shot." The people in the chapel laugh as he begins to read the obituary I wrote for Josh. Before long, I start to worry that his mispronunciation of names is bordering on disrespect, and I make my way to the podium in true control-freak style.

"Want some help?" I say as I approach him, and a little more laughter breaks out. The lightheartedness is a good thing. Standing at the front of the room, I see the full range of people who have come. Some are sitting in the aisles between pews. Behind the pews to the back of the chapel is standing room only. The doors of the chapel are propped open, and the speakers have been turned on so that a lobby full of people can hear the service. I finish reading the names, and the officiant gives me the nod to begin my eulogy.

. . .

"On July 9, 1990, I pushed a beautiful little boy into the world. Twenty-three years, nine months, and twenty-one days later, we are here to say good-bye to him. Over the past several days, I have barely slept or eaten. There have been times when I've forgotten to breathe. But being with you brings me comfort. I will never understand his death, but, through each of you, I know his life had meaning. Thank you all for being here."

Tears well in my eyes. I have to blink to see the words written on the paper.

"Today, I want to share with you three lessons I learned about life from my son. Things that I believe make my life more meaningful. The title of this eulogy is: 'What Would Joshua Do?' Number one: you can never have too much of a good thing."

I talk about Joshua's contagious enthusiasm for life. How he put his whole heart into everything he did. From soccer to lacrosse to writing poetry to working on motorcycles. How I paid for his first tattoo for his eighteenth birthday—a customized piece with the initials and birthdays of his father and his grandfather—and three months later, he had five tattoos, including the one with the names of his sisters and another with the names of his parents. How he was thinking about buying a Harley, and, a few months later, he not only owned a Harley and had embraced being a rider all the way to his bones, but he also worked at the dealership where he'd bought the bike.

"When Joshua loved, he loved abundantly," I say, and go on, "Number two: some things are worth fighting for."

Starting from the third grade, I got a call every year from his school saying my son had been in a fight. The first time, he'd beaten up a kid for making fun of a classmate with cerebral palsy. Years later at college, he was expelled for beating up a kid who was talking bad about his mother. The fact that the kid had never met me was of no matter. Joshua knew what he stood for, and he defended it fiercely.

"Number three: nothing matters more than family."

By this time, my knees have stopped shaking. What I am saying is perhaps the most important message I will ever give. I go off script and speak from my heart.

"Many of you have been around us the past few days. But even if you are just joining us for the first time today, you might have noticed that we don't use words like 'step' or 'half' when we talk about our relationship to one another. We are family.

"Some people find it strange, but Joshua felt that sense of family that wrapped him in love, and he shared it with others.

"Look around you today. Look at the people in this room. Not just at the people you came with, look a couple of pews over."

People start to look around the room.

"Look in the back of the room."

Motorcycle riders from every walk of life stand in the back of the room.

"Look at the people sitting on the floor in the aisles," I say.

Josh's friends fill the space between the seats.

"We are white, black, Hispanic, and Asian. There are people dressed in biker leathers. There are people in three-piece suits. Women in sequined church hats and others with bandanas in their hair. There are gay people, lesbian people, transgender people, and every other point on the spectrum. There are Christians, Buddhists, atheists, and Jews.

"*See* that. And then see the human spirit in each one of these people that Joshua recognized and honored as his family.

"Twenty-three years, nine months, and twenty-one days. We were so fortunate for every minute of the time that we shared the earth with Joshua. I hope each one of you carries his spirit with you for the rest of your life. Recognize the human spirit that lives in each person you meet. Even when—especially when—they are different from you.

"Love. Only love. Always love."

12

"Some of us are going to shred tires at the site of the accident if you want to go." Felipe is weighed down with grief. Instead of a happy, joking young man, he looks tired and depleted. Felipe and his brother, Miguel, have been best friends with Joshua all their lives. They've gone through boyhood problems, adolescent problems, and manhood problems together and remained as close as brothers.

"What does that mean, shred tires?"

"Well," Felipe answers, "it's . . . um . . . just what it sounds like. We go to the site and spin our back tires until they blow up."

Neither Noè nor I have been to the site, for all the reasons you might imagine. I am afraid there is blood on the pavement. I'm afraid I will feel the fear and pain that he felt at the moment of the accident. But I have found peace in unexpected places in the past few days, and, inside, I do want to see the place where my son took his last breath.

"I'll go," I say.

Bill, Claudia, and I make it to the site before Felipe and the other riders. Twenty people are already gathered around a five-foot purple cross that rises over a vacant lot. The words "Fly High" are painted on the cross in red. There are sunflowers, white carnations, and roses. Prayer candles. And a long piece of laminate covered with messages from friends and family in colored marker. There are empty cans where Joshua's friends have stopped by to have a beer with him. Some have tied their bandanas around the cross. There is no blood.

Left from the accident's investigation is a dotted line of orange spray paint running over the railroad tracks and ending at a concrete utility pole twenty yards or so away. A stick figure is drawn on the pavement along with the letters "PPOR"—person's place of rest. I try to imagine him lying there, but I quickly push the image away. Instead, I lie down on the pavement with my face against the street like his face would have been. I try to feel him there. Was he still conscious when he lay here? Was he in pain?

"Look!" Noè says as I move from the pavement to the curb. He points at the sky as a white dove circles the site, then lands on the telephone wire across the street.

I stare in astonishment. It's hard not to feel that there is meaning to this universal symbol of peace showing up just as we gathered at the site of the accident.

Soon, Harley-Davidsons come over the tracks with a bubbling roar and position themselves with front tires against the curb over the painted stick figure.

Felipe's head drops as he leads the pack in a loud acceleration.

"The last rev," someone whispers to me. "It's a tradition," she says, and I nod.

Following Felipe's lead, each rider stands to straddle his bike, and rear tires spit hot smoke and squeal against the street. After a few minutes, the heat and friction become too much, and, one by one, the tires bust in a puff of smoke, and we all cheer.

After the ritual, the riders take spare tires from the back of a pickup truck and begin replacing the ones that have been decimated. Noè's eyes haven't moved from the dove that still watches over us from the wire above the scene.

"That dove is Joshua," he tells me, shaking his head. "It sure is. That's my boy. I can't believe it."

Neither can I. I'm worried that if I move the bird might fly away. Then again, it sat right there through the noise and the smoke. Noè walks slowly toward the bird while I hold my breath. Standing under the dove, he looks up and opens his arms.

"Hello, *mijo*," he says. "I love you."

The bird opens his wings and flaps them as if to say, "Hi, Dad. I love you too."

. . .

It's time to go back to Michigan. We have to find our new normal, even though it feels like our lives are at a standstill. Claudia has to finish her sophomore year of high school, and Bill needs to get seeds in the ground if we're going to grow food this year. I crave the quiet open space and sky at night with no interference from streetlights or city noise. I crave home.

Memphis is not my home anymore. I have no love lost for this city. The desperation here is so thick it sticks to your skin. There is so much poverty. So much fear. And, if it's possible for a city to be in a perpetual state of anger, Memphis is. White people are angry that black people won't just act like them and stop making everyone so uncomfortable. Black people are angry that white people don't understand why they were ever angry in the first place. Everyone is afraid Latinos will take their jobs. It's been years since Martin Luther King Jr. was murdered here, but the people who live in Memphis know that not much has changed.

When I moved to Michigan, I left with almost no regrets. Almost.

"We are leaving tomorrow," I type out a text to Kimberly. She has chosen to spend most of her time surrounded by friends rather than family, and I feel like I've hardly seen her since we arrived. It will be hard to leave her and Michael. Leaving them now feels like I'm walking away when they need me most. When I need *them* most. I vow to come back soon. She sends me a sad face.

"Mom," she texts, "Michael said he talked to Joshua last night." That doesn't surprise me. Talking to a child seems exactly like what Josh would do. And, I'm intrigued.

"Can I call him?" I ask. Since she only uses the text function, actual phone calls require prior notice or they won't be answered. I'm almost giggly from wanting to hear Michael tell me what they talked about.

"Sure. He is spending the night with Nana tonight. You can call him there."

Panic immediately sucks me up into a tight knot. I've never considered my mother's house to be a safe place for anyone who couldn't fend for himself. But maybe things have changed. She was lucid at Joshua's funeral after all. And I know how much joy Michael brings to the house. We could all use a little joy. Would I begrudge my mother that joy just after her grandson died?

I dial my mother's number.

When she answers, I hear cartoons in the background.

"How are you holding up?" she asks me, and I tell her I'm okay. Ready to go home.

She tells me she has a few things to give me. A diary that belonged to Mamaw and a few trinkets from when I was a baby. She says she loves me. There was a time when I would hang up the phone before she could say those words. I was unable to hold that information alongside the pain of my childhood. But something in me has softened. "I love you too," I say, and she hands the phone to Michael.

"Hi, Grandma."

When I hear his voice, I think about the last five years that he and his mother have lived with us. Our weekend trips to the diner to eat pancakes and to the thrift store to buy a toy. How he would come to my bed for a story, then pretend he was asleep when his mother came to get him.

"I'll be back to see you soon, okay?" I tell him. Soon is good enough for him. He wants to get back to his cartoons.

"Grandma?" he says.

"Yes, my love?" God, I love this kid.

"Josh said tell you not to worry. He's spending the night with me tonight."

I worry anyway. At four a.m., I wake sweating with my heart beating in my ears. All the things that could go wrong flash through my mind. Has my mother fallen asleep with a cigarette in her hand and caught the house on fire? Are the doors locked so that Michael won't go outside? I am barely able to wait until the sun comes up before I drive to her house.

Mama doesn't live far from the neighborhood where I grew up. It has reinvented itself every ten years or so as long as I can remember. The houses are small—built for soldiers returning from World War II—with tidy yards planted in buttercups and detached one-car garages. By the eighties, many of the original owners had moved, having either left their starter homes to their children or rented them out. Little by little, the yards became less tidy, and by Y2K the buttercups had been replaced with cars on cinder blocks and worn-out living room furniture.

Mama's house has not burned to the ground as I feared. It's there, all right, blending right into the naked bleakness of the neighborhood. The sun is barely up, and skinny dogs are pawing through trash bags left on the curb. Plywood covers broken windowpanes. Scarcity. Deprivation. I park on the street and watch for a few minutes, my heart pounding.

This is crazy. I'm stalking my own mother. Is the fear irrational? I'll get something to eat, then decide whether to knock on the door.

Thirty minutes later, I pull into Mama's driveway and get out of my car. Through the screen door, I can see my mother sitting on her bed drinking a cup of coffee. Michael is cuddled up to her, sleeping like a rock. I gather all my cool, tap on the screen door, then go inside.

Mama's house is dark with nicotine-stained walls. No window has been opened to let in light or let out the stale, heavy air. Aisles lead through stacks and stacks of stuff from the living room to her bedroom, where my precious grandson lies sleeping.

"I was . . ."

What was I doing? I was having an anxiety attack. I was afraid Michael was dead. I was afraid that the single most terrifying thing I can imagine, that this . . . this atrocity, this unjust blow of death could happen again, to Michael this time, and there would not be a damned thing I could do about it.

"I just wanted to see Michael," I say, barely finishing before I collapse, sobbing into my grandson's sleeping body.

Mama rubs the top of my head. "Come lay next to Mom," she tells me, and for a moment my fear of needing my mama and her not being there disappears. I curve my body around Michael's, lay my head on the bed next to my mother, and fall asleep.

When I wake up, my mother is in the kitchen making another pot of coffee. The fear has returned. I'm aware of the danger of staying too long. Of keeping my guard down long enough for things to go wrong. This is my chance to make a quick break. I yell over my shoulder, "I'm gone," and slip out the door just as a dove leaves the roof of my mother's house and flies into the horizon.

I wonder if I'm going insane. Each day has brought me another sign from my son.

I don't believe in signs.

But how else can I explain the birds? The doves. And the hummingbird on Noë's patio.

It's probably a well-documented phenomenon of grief. The brain interprets normal, everyday things in a way that brings relief. My mind is playing tricks on me to make me feel better.

I get in my car and head back to Noë's house to pack for home.

13

Back in Michigan, the summer passes in a blur. From the beginning, Bill has laid low. But when I need something, I look up, and there he is with whatever I need. Food. Comfort. A glass of wine. My days are spent staring out the window watching the birds come and go. Mourning doves gather under the evergreen trees and seem to have nested in the barn just beyond. Hummingbirds come to the feeder outside the window where I write. Have they always been here? Is it merely a change in my own perspective that brings them into my consciousness several times a day?

My brain is filled with questions. Should I move back to Memphis? Kimberly and Michael are there now, and so is Alicia. The memorial at the site of Joshua's accident is there. Noè and Michele are there—the only people who come close to understanding how I feel. And being around people who share my love for Joshua helps combat the doldrums.

Or should I move to the beach where the sound of the waves can calm the fisted knot that's a constant presence in my chest? Maybe Michigan's Upper Peninsula, so I can hike and play in Lake Superior with my German shepherd, Ezra.

I get out of bed most days. On good days, I cook a meal for my family. Brushing my teeth and showering are still more than I can manage. I understand how people lose it—go off the deep end and never return.

Sometimes I feel like I will too. I sit on my therapist's couch with my legs tucked under me, looking for a way to explain how I feel.

"Have you ever dropped acid?" I ask her. The days just after Joshua died were like that. Everything was in vivid detail, and the world moved more slowly. For those few days, I felt connected to something important. Something bigger than me. When I looked at the sky, I saw the colors on parts of the spectrum usually hidden from human eyes. I heard the song of every bird that had ever sung and the musical notes that composers heard in their dreams. I was plugged in to something so real and so magnificent, and it kept me grounded in the knowledge that no matter how devastating this moment was it was also sacred.

And then, it stopped. And there was nothing but pain where it had been.

Throughout my life, I've had moments like these only in glimpses. Seeing children be born. Watching the waterfalls on the Presque Isle River in the Upper Peninsula. It's a sense of wonder snuggled up tightly with a sense of being so minuscule that you might not be of any significance at all. For some, that feeling of being just a fleck of stardust is fearsome. But for me, it's amazing. I once used a yardstick as an example to tell my children what I meant.

"Imagine this yardstick represents everything that exists anywhere," I said. All the stars and planets. All the animals, plants, and minerals. Gases and liquids. And this centimeter right here," I said, pointing somewhere between the fifth and sixth inches, "this represents all of what human beings currently know and understand."

The idea that what is out there to know is so much more vast than what I currently know—or what anyone currently knows—frees me.

It's hard not to use the word "God" to explain what I felt after Joshua's death. But for me, the word, especially when it's capitalized, evokes the idea of a man with a white beard sitting somewhere up high. Apart and away from us, choreographing our destinies and punishing sinners. Separate and away from me doesn't come close to what I felt. Controlling and punishing, even less so. This energy was *in* me. Ran *through* me. And it connected me not only to every other living being on earth but to the atoms on planets my feeble human mind could not even fathom. It was beautiful and profound. Breathtaking and calming. And I believe it was the only thing that got me through the days just after Joshua died.

Some of the things that have happened since Joshua died have been so bizarre that I haven't been able to talk about them in polite company. Some of them have fit better with society's generally accepted idea of God and death, and those are easier to talk about. Other things, though, leave me wondering whether they really happened the way I remember them or if my mind is playing tricks on me.

The day Joshua died, for example, was less than a month after my forty-seventh birthday. My body had started to change in ways that were foreign to me—my skin was drier, my eyesight more strained—and I was journaling about it regularly. For months leading up to that day, my menstrual cycle was all but nonexistent. If my periods came at all, they were light and lasted just long enough to be annoying.

On the day that Joshua died—and at the exact time listed as the time of death, I was meeting with the rest of my team at the small community hospital where I worked. As the room got warmer, someone asked me to open the window. When I stood up, though, my uterus emptied itself. Blood soaked through my clothes and into the cushion of the chair I was sitting in.

Five hours before my brain became aware, my body wept for my dead child.

Maybe that was a coincidence. Maybe the dove that joined us at the site of Joshua's accident was a coincidence. Or maybe, coincidence is how we define things that fall outside of our centimeter of understanding.

.   .   .

My dreams are intense and vacillate between terrifying and grounding. I often dream about Joshua, and, in some cases, I wake up feeling like we've just visited. Other dreams, though, transform my waking thoughts into distorted images like a funhouse mirror.

One day, I heard an interview on the radio about cremation. Apparently, after a person is cremated, the only things left as ash are bone fragments. Everything that was regenerating and alive—muscle, skin, organs—is decimated by the fire that sometimes reaches eighteen hundred degrees. The thought of how Joshua's body looked as it went through that process pops into my head from time to time, but my brain is kind enough to quickly push it away. Sometimes, though, it sneaks into my dreams.

In the dream, I'm chanting, "Ashes, ashes. My son's ashes," and twirling around in the grass behind my house holding Joshua's marble urn. As I twirl, I unscrew the top of the urn and pour the ashes over my body.

My fingers run through the cool powder. It is fine and soft, like the cornstarch Mamaw used to pat on my chubby thighs when they rubbed together and made a raw place. I rub the ashes around in my palm with my index finger, making small circles that get bigger and bigger until there is a thin sheen over my hand. Then I rub my hands together. Now, they both shine with my son's light. I rub my hands on my forearms, then on my face. I raise my hands to my face and inhale my son's essence. I lick my hand and taste the bitterness of all that is left of him on earth, spinning until I collapse dizzy onto the grass.

When I wake up, I feel dirty and dark and like I never, ever want to sleep again.

14

It is after I wake up from one of these dreams and I'm in my kitchen making tea when the text from my sister comes.

"Mom is in the emergency room. Her heart stopped in the ambulance. They won't let us back to see her."

My guts clench. Mama ends up in the emergency room a lot. Most of the time, she's either taken too many pain pills or is out of them and suffering from withdrawal. And most of the time, they give her a prescription just to get rid of her. Mama has been flagged as a drug seeker in every ER in town.

But her heart stopping—that could be something serious. Her own mother died of ovarian cancer. Her grandmother died of heart problems. I'm almost afraid to know.

I wait an hour, then type, "How's she doing?"

Jessica responds quickly. "She was full of Xanax and morphine. They pumped her stomach."

It's not cancer. Of course it's not.

My ears ring with hate. What a fool I was for letting my guard down. For ever thinking that things might have changed. For thinking that her grandson dying might be the kick in the ass she needed. For thinking that she might really be sick this time. Just like all the other times before, she'll be fine. She'll say she wasn't trying to kill herself, she just lost track of what she'd taken. She'll promise to do better and only take her pills according to the doctor's orders. And then, she'll slink back into the routine of living off pills and black coffee and burning holes in her mattress when she passes out. Jessica says she's talking about going into a detox program to get clean—a state which I predict will last exactly seventy-two hours from when she is discharged.

In my bed, I pull the quilt up to my chin. Maybe sleep would be a good thing after all.

I dream that I sit cross-legged on her bed. Her arms are crossed, and she's holding a cigarette between swollen fingers with nails brown from nicotine. She won't look at me, but her expression says she's perturbed I'm here.

"If someone really wants to die," I tell her, "there are much more efficient ways to do it." Out of my backpack, I pull a .22 revolver—the one I use if a rattler and I cross paths on a hike—and lay it on her bed.

"It's a little more messy, but it's over quickly. C'mon. Do us all a favor." I push it toward her.

She looks at me defiantly. "You really want me to kill myself, don't you?" She takes a long drag off her cigarette and talks while she holds the smoke in her lungs. "What kind of shit is this?" she says. "My own daughter wants me to die." She nods to herself as ashes fall on the front of her coffee-stained T-shirt.

"What I *want*," I scream, "is a fucking break! What I *want* is for you to stop torturing yourself and everyone around you." Tears run hot down my face.

"Years ago, I wanted you to stop using and be my mother. Now, I just want to not be afraid that you'll burn the house down and kill everyone in it. Or that someone will find you after you've been dead for days and you've seeped and soaked the mattress.

"Do the decent thing. Just. Fucking. Do it."

She says okay in a way that sounds like she's giving in. She picks up the pistol, aims it right between my eyes, and shoots me dead.

.   .   .

At work, I try to put on a happy face and be productive even though my focus and concentration are nonexistent. Getting back to normal feels like looking for something that isn't there. I need a new sense of normal, and it's up to me to figure out what that is.

Since I spent four months after we returned from Memphis measuring my days based on whether I got out of bed, showing up to work and making it through a workday feels like a win. Slowly, projects are returned to me by the people who filled in while I was out. Some days I nap in my car or work through lunch so I can leave early and nap at home, hoping that will give me the energy to make dinner for Bill and Claudia. Every single moment, I am thinking of Joshua. His absence is all-consuming.

One day my boss asks, "What is your plan for pulling it together?" There's an innocent smile on her face, and her head is tilted to the side the way a puppy does when whining for a treat. She holds the smile as my head spins.

It's only been a few months since Joshua died. I don't even know what pulling it together looks like, much less how to make a plan to get there. My head swirls, and my chest tightens. I am in a corner, and there is only one way out.

"You'll have my resignation on your desk on Monday," I say.

I am a constant reminder of something people would rather not deal with. I am walking darkness with a stain on my shirt. I'm late and rude, and my hair is unwashed. The part of me that understood social niceties is lost. I am raw and starting to putrefy, and I don't have the power to stop it.

There's a play by Sophocles about a soldier who gets wounded in battle. The soldier's wound is terribly painful, grotesque to look at, and smells awful. The other soldiers abandon him in the night because of it.

Grieving is like that. At first, people were sad because I was sad. Joshua's death made them consider for a moment that their children could also die. But that's hard to sit with for very long, so, with time, they eased back into a place that's less painful. It couldn't really happen to them. Secretly they believe that someone *must* have done something to make this happen. Young men don't just die on their lunch break on a clear, sunny Wednesday afternoon. It's at that point my open wound starts to reek. Their sadness turns to pity because I haven't moved on. They wish I would find something to talk about other than my son's death. Some of them go away.

I would go away too if I could.

I pity them too. I pity them because I know something that most people will pass through their entire lives without fully understanding. That thing is this: Children die every day. And life goes on. It won't be the same as it was, but the sun will rise and set, and babies will be born, and the earth will keep turning.

I know that when people ask me, "Why Joshua?" they could just as easily ask, "Why not Joshua?" He was no more treasured by those who love him than anyone else. No more important than the Muslim men murdered in Bosnia or the children who died from Ebola in Sierra Leone. No more special than the children lost to the streets.

I know that it could happen to them. And that they would wake up the next day and go on living in a world they once thought they understood. It's cruel and it's disgusting, but life goes on.

. . .

My bathtub can be filled three times before the water heater in the basement is empty. After that, I have to keep all of my skin under the water and out of the chilled, drafty bathroom. I can hear the old window rattle against the wind. I shiver and slide down the tub until my head is underwater.

The watery lens blurs the view of my bathroom. The black shower curtain with big red roses hanging along the rings. There's a print of a self-portrait by Frida Kahlo with hemostats pinched around her severed artery over the towel rack. Every day, I look for a reason to stay here. Today, I haven't found it.

Razors, a pink one and one with a purple swirl, hang from a rack. They are old, probably even rusted. This is the kind of thing a person wants to get right the first time. A new razor would be required if I were to go through with it.

I ask for a sign, but there is nothing but the drip of the faucet making waves in my ears. I think about my living children, and I know they will feel I didn't love them enough to stay here. They won't understand that losing even one of them busted a hole in me so large that there isn't enough of me left to piece together. I cannot heal from this wound. It will kill me. This is terminal. Dying no longer frightens me. In the past, I have fought with everything in me to stay alive. Now it feels like a zero-sum game. This side or the other, I can handle either one.

I've been fooling myself. Telling myself that the birds, the dreams, the songs on the radio, are messages from the other side. And maybe they are. But I don't want messages.

I don't want dreams.

I don't want signs.

I want my fucking son.

15

How can I explain something so devastating as losing a child? Do the words even exist? And if so, in what language? How many ways can I say "I am sad" before it sounds trite and meaningless? Grief pulls me inward, to the bottom of my soul, to dark places down deep where all my monsters live and I can't breathe. When I think I can't take it anymore, it holds me under a little longer. Instead of clear, life-giving air, I only suck in more darkness when I breathe. When the thought enters my mind that I myself will soon die, I feel relieved. I don't want to live in a world that doesn't have my son in it. And, just when my mind is made up, grief releases me to float back to the surface and wait to endure the next wave.

People who say it gets better with time are misinformed. It never gets better, it only gets different. I still wake up missing my son and go to bed looking for answers. I dream that I am lying on the soft leather seat of a limousine. I'm confused and impatient—like I'm looking for something I know is there but I cannot find. Driving the car is a man with long gray hair, and, though I can only see him from the back, I know that he is a good man and someone who can help me make sense of things.

"Where are we going?" I ask him without sitting up.

"To find what you're looking for," he tells me. Then, he holds up his right hand as a map of Michigan and points to the top of his index finger.

"On the bay?" I ask, and he nods yes.

. . .

The next morning, I pull out my atlas. The state of Michigan is shaped like a right hand held up with the palm turned outward. We live in the meaty pad just below the thumb. About three hundred miles away, Cheboygan State Park is on the Straits of Mackinac, just where the index and middle finger meet. Grass Bay is nearby. It's a rainy October, and the weather will be chilly, but I feel pulled to follow this dream wherever it may take me.

"I need some time alone," I tell Bill. "Do some writing. Be near the water." He looks at me cautiously.

I answer what I assume to be his unspoken question with: "I've got money." I book the smallest cabin at a resort nearby. What does someone take on a trip to find what they are looking for? Into my duffel bag, I stuff three T-shirts, a flannel shirt, and a pair of jeans. Hiking boots, my notebook, and a used copy of a Kerouac novel.

I watch the leaves change as I drive north. When I lose my radio station, I turn off the radio and ride in silence, except for the sound of my tires on the road.

It's evening when I arrive at my cabin, and it's started to rain. Two hundred and fifty square feet with red-and-white-checkered curtains over windows that open on hinges. A bed, a sink, a refrigerator. A shower and a toilet have been added in the back. There's a television, but the rain has knocked out the cable and Internet connection, so distortion is the only thing available to watch. The rain on the roof lulls me to sleep. I shiver under quilts handmade by people I don't know and sleep in my favorite wool thrift store sweater—the same one I was wearing the night we drove to Memphis.

The next morning, I pull out my notebook and plan my day: buy coffee, write, find the bay. By the time I'm ready to leave the cabin, the rain has stopped, but the air is still misty. I can hear the waves of Paradise Lake hitting the shore.

I buy coffee at a small grocery store that was once a log cabin. An old golden retriever lopes by the front door and raises one eyebrow at me as I pass. I head north—the route will take me to Mackinaw City, the very point of the index finger—before I turn south and drive along the Michigan shoreline for another thirty miles. The lake peeks through evergreen trees and then opens up just as I see a sign telling me I've reached Grass Bay. The only lakes I ever knew of as a child were muddy and smelled like dead fish, but not the Great Lakes. Lake Huron is deep blue, and you can't see the other side from the shore. Beach grass grows tall and piping plovers nest there, leaving tiny gray-and-black-speckled eggs in shallow depressions in the sand. Waves have washed over rocks until they are flat and smooth. Near the dock, a gray-haired woman paints on an easel, dressed in a long skirt and a scarf, a straw hat tied under her chin.

I think about the water and all the little living things that are in it. How we are like the grains of sand getting washed back and forth from water to earth and back to water.

The water almost reaches the log I sit on, so I take off my shoes and bury my toes in the wet sand. The water makes me feel so small, like a grain of sand. And if I am a grain of sand, then maybe Joshua was too. Maybe it was time for him to return to where he came from, to return to the dust from which he was made. Maybe the only answer is that there *is* no answer.

With a stick, I write Joshua's name in the sand. For minutes, the waves barely reach it and take away only the tiniest part of his name. Then, a larger wave washes over his entire name, leaving only shallow trenches where the letters have been. Then, the final wave comes and leaves the sand smooth.

As the water recedes, the smooth surface starts to differentiate into individual grains of sand. Pebbles become apparent, shells. Where it looked like the waves took everything away, left nothing, no pebble, no shell, not one thing of beauty or importance, I now see life.

I lie down in the grass and fall asleep.

.   .   .

I still wake up missing my son every day. There are two things I remember repeating in the moments right after I got the call saying Joshua had died. One was "My son." The other was "What am I going to do?" My life had exploded into millions of pieces, and the world expected me to put them back together. To remember how to breathe in and out and go on living. Grief hits you like a blow to the head—you have to learn to talk again, eat again, walk again. How to live in the strange new world without your child.

As I think back on that day, I can't tell you how I felt. Sure, there was pain. The kind that roots itself in your chest and grows bigger every time your heart beats and your child's does not. Yet, the word "pain" is too weak and abstract. And, it's not just loss, though certainly a piece of you is missing. Loneliness isn't quite the word, but you miss your child every minute of every day. Then there's regret, guilt, and anger. No one word adequately describes how it feels. At the same time, all the words in every language that has ever existed aren't enough to describe it.

And feeling is not the only level at which you experience the loss of a child. You also experience it physically. Intellectually. Spiritually. You cease to move through the world the way you did the second before it happened. It changes you on a molecular level. And you know it. And you carry the knowledge that you are changed every day. The people you talk to during the day, the woman in the checkout line at the grocery store, the kid selling M&M's door-to-door for his Boy Scouts troop, they can't tell. But you know it. You also know that, even if you tried to explain it to them, they would not understand. You are an alien. A foreign being learning how to live on a planet of people whose children are still alive.

Only . . .

People die every day. *Children* die every day.

And mothers go on. They go on seeking shelter from bombs. They go on praying for an end to disease. They go on waiting for the rainy season to end. They go on, without the privilege of mourning. My sisters, they go on. And that gives me strength. In the end—when our ashes have been scattered and our graves have been filled—what is left of us is our story. How we lived and how we died and the people we touched along the way.

I am proud of Joshua's story. Every little bit of it. I'm proud I had a son who rode a Harley. I'm proud that he had the names of the people who meant the most to him permanently inked on his body. I'm proud that he stood up for those who couldn't stand up for themselves. I'm proud of the man who cried every time he watched *The Notebook* and loved *The Lion King* best of all. I'm proud that he was a person who knew what he stood for and wasn't afraid to let other people know.

And, I want to become proud of my story too.

The pain may never go away, but maybe it can exist alongside something more. Strength. Resilience. Maybe I can honor my struggle for what it has taught me. Maybe I can teach others a little of what I have learned.

Love. Only love. Always love.

16

It's winter now in southeast Michigan, seven months after Joshua's funeral, and snow covers the ground of our farm. Claudia is midway through her junior year of high school, and Kimberly and Michael are all settled in Tennessee. The hummingbirds have been replaced with cardinals, but the mourning doves have stayed for the winter and leave footprints in the snow outside my door.

Things are back to normal with Mama. The bubble of compassion that cushioned us from each other after Joshua's death has deflated, and our default ways of being are back in play. Her sadness has dissolved into depression. Depression is relieved with self-medication. Self-medication feeds her addiction. And addiction requires isolation to exist.

Something inside me has changed. Softened. If I've learned anything from Joshua's death, it is this: all we really have is this moment. And each moment is precious. The moments when I met my mother head-on in our grief and stood there with her were precious. And I'm working to hold on as tightly to those memories as I hold on to the more difficult ones.

Soon, it will be the first anniversary of Joshua's death, though it seems like it happened just yesterday. I still think of him every moment of every day, but my memories now make me smile more than they make me cry.

I still run through the scenario of his accident—the sunny Wednesday afternoon, the lone utility pole, the way neither Joshua's body nor his motorcycle suffered any visible physical damage. Every time I go through the moment just before he wrecks, I believe for an instant it will turn out differently.

A few months before Joshua died, I was looking at one of my favorite pictures of him. It was taken at a department store kiosk when he was three years old. He's posed on a table wearing white shorts and a red-white-and-blue-striped Guess T-shirt and holding a ball.

The night when I looked at that picture, I cried. I turned my head for a second and my sweet, silly little boy had grown into a man. I wished I had realized how quickly it was all going to pass and spent more time savoring those moments. I've felt the same way looking at pictures of my girls too.

Now, I find myself sitting in my kitchen with the winter light coming through the windows looking at a picture of Joshua taken by his sister Kelsi less than twenty-four hours before he died. He had gone to his dad's house after work to finish a welding project. When he'd gotten there, instead of going out to the garage to work, he said to Kelsi, "Let's take a nap." She snapped a picture of him sleeping—looking as peaceful and content with life as any man on earth ever looked.

We won't ever capture that moment again.

But the truth is, we won't ever capture *any* of the moments of his life again. Or any of the moments of any of our lives. Every second, each one of us is changing. The atoms that make up our bodies are dying, and new ones are coming into existence. Just like Joshua will never again be that little boy holding the ball again, he'll never again be that man asleep in his Bumpus Harley-Davidson shirt again.

Moments pass. All of them.

People change. All of them.

Even though I never expected this to be a spiritual journey for me, it is proving to be just that, in a very real way. I'm learning that there are things that I can't see or hear or touch that are just as real as the old pine table I'm sitting at right now. Like ultraviolet light, the sound of a dog whistle, or a magnetic field.

I still don't know where God fits into this picture for me, but here's what I do know: everything that was my son has always existed and continues to exist. When the smoke from the crematorium went through that smokestack, it carried all the elements of his physical body out into the world. It hangs there in a fine mist, and you and I breathe him in the air and touch him in the rain. The sun shines through him and all those who've gone before us.

Acknowledgments

Thanks to . . .

My husband, Bill Bass. I told you I didn't know how to be a wife, and you told me to just be myself. Thank you for believing in me.

The Muñoz family. Thank you for giving me the space to process our loss through writing.

My sister, Jessica, who has always been my biggest fan.

A special thanks to . . .

My editing team: Anne Horowitz, Nancy Koziol, Nancy Owens Nelson, and Candice Gideon. *Wailing Wall* is a better book because of you, and I couldn't have done it without you.

Everyone who backed *Wailing Wall* with your money, time, and energy. This book is an act of community and love.

About the Author

Deedra Climer is a Southern writer who'd rather write about race and poverty than sweet tea and magnolias. Born and raised in Memphis, she splits her time between Tennessee and southeast Michigan, where she runs a small organic farm and apiary with her daughter Claudia and husband, Bill.

List of Patrons

This book was made possible in part by the following grand patrons who preordered the book on Inkshares.com. Thank you.

Andrew J. Hromadka
Angelica Tejeda
Anne Farrand
Cameron R. Getto
Cary and Gabi Scarbrough
Debbie A. Hale
Denise R. Bennett
Georgina Hickey
H. P. Chatham
Janice L. Person
Jason and Sheila Climer
Jeni Chatham
Jessica Grisham
Jessica Kilbourn
Judy Kumher
Kathleen Hodges

Kristen Ziel
Kristi G. Stamey
Melissa Rosenblum
Michael Wayne Hankins Jr.
Mona Lea
Monroe Martial Arts
Nancy E. Delaney
Peggy Yanke
Rebecca Wauldron
Stacey L. Fallis
Timothy W. Bumps
Tracey Harris
Vicki Grisham
Wendy Diaz

And many others who supported *Wailing Wall* with time, energy, money, and love.

Inkshares

Inkshares is a crowdfunded book publisher. We democratize publishing by having readers select the books we publish—we edit, design, print, distribute, and market any book that meets a preorder threshold.

Interested in making a book idea come to life? Visit inkshares.com to find new book projects or to start your own.